Exploring a The Celebrations

How and why are religious festivals important?

Religious festivals matter deeply to many people. In countries around the world religious festivals are huge cultural events and family occasions which express shared beliefs and values, and a sense of identity and commitment.

Exploring religious festivals is a popular activity in RE. It is engaging, colourful and active; full of story and artefacts; music, food and enjoyment! But we will be missing the point, and doing the children a disservice, if we only pay attention to the outward expression and give insufficient time to an exploration of the inner meaning.

Good RE does not stop after considering the 'How' – but gives plenty of opportunity and structure to enable children to engage with the 'Why'. It is only then that children will glimpse something special – the 'treasure that lies beneath the surface' – a deepening of understanding and awareness of what it is to be human, and of what really matters most in life.

This is at the heart of all religious festivals. Are you prepared to help your children explore? This publication suggests some practical strategies to help your children on this exciting voyage of discovery!

Joyce Mackley
Editor

RE Today weblink:
www.retoday.org.uk

The RE Today website provides some free additional resources and classroom ready materials for subscribers. Look out for the 'RE Today on the web' logo at the end of selected articles.

The password for access can be found in each term's REtoday magazine.

Age	Contents	Page
	What's in a religious festival? Joyce Mackley	2-4
4-7	Using song to engage children with a religious festival (Succot: Judaism) Joyce Mackley	5-7
5-7	Using dance to engage children with a religious festival (Navrati: Hinduism) Joyce Mackley	8-9
5-7	Using an artefact to explore a religious festival (Eid ul Fitr: Islam) Victoria Ikuemesi	10-12
5-7	Using story and pictures to explore a religious festival (Easter: Christianity) Joyce Mackley	13-15
7-11	Bringing Easter alive: an Easter Labyrinth Peter Greaves	16-20
7-11	Celebrating Divali: Hindu and Sikh perspectives Rosemary Rivett	21-26
9-11	Hanukkah: what's the real meaning of this Jewish festival? Lat Blaylock	28-33

What's in a religious festival?

For the teacher:

Why teach festivals?
Festivals are...
- outward manifestations of religious faith
- shared experiences
- expressions of the human need to have 'high days' and 'holidays' to celebrate things of significance and value in our lives
- celebrations of personal and community identity: the marking of events which say something about who we are and what matters to us.

What do we need to remember and to avoid?
- Avoid only looking at the external features, the things people do and say or eat.
- Explore 'why' people keep special days and times of year. As teachers, we always need to keep in mind the question 'What do we want pupils to *learn from* religious festivals?' The chart below identifies some important aspects and some examples from three religions.

Planning
Religious festivals express the beliefs and values that matter most to a faith community. When planning a unit on how and why people celebrate religious festivals it is important to include the following four aspects.

Shared story
Remembering significant events, for example:
Divali: the return of Rama and Sita as told in the epic poem, the *Ramayana* (Hindu) /release of Guru Har Gobind from prison (Sikh)
Christmas: the birth of Jesus
Eid ul Fitr: remembering the first revelation of the Qur'an to Muhammad.

Shared beliefs
A living expression of beliefs, for example:
Divali: the welcoming of Lakshmi, the goddess of wealth and prosperity
Christmas: expressing a belief in God becoming human in Jesus (incarnation)
Eid ul Fitr: expressing thanks to Allah for the gift of self-control during Ramadan.

Shared values
Festivals are ways of passing on the beliefs and values that matter most to a community.

Shared hopes
Expressing hope for the future, for example:
Divali for blessings and good fortune in the new year; good defeating evil (Hindu)
Christmas: for peace and goodwill for all
Eid ul Fitr: for forgiveness, harmony, community.

Shared commitments
A renewal of commitment, for example:
Divali: to strive for courage and freedom (Sikh)
Christmas: to follow Jesus' teaching and example
Eid ul Fitr: to be faithful, generous and help the needy.

Getting started
The use of a strategy to encourage children to talk about and around festivals and celebrations, asking questions and looking for meaning is an important starting point for learning in this topic in all age groups. The activity offered on page 4, using the cards opposite, is one way of doing this.

Sorting out celebrations: a card and discussion activity for all

Introduction: This activity uses the cards on page 3 to support paired talk.

Objectives: With structured follow-up discussion, this activity will help pupils to consider how the celebrations of a faith community are similar to, and different from, personal celebrations. The activity could be used at the start of a unit exploring religious festivals to make links with children's own experience and to involve children in planning their future learning.

Resources: You will need one pack of cards for each pair, copied and cut up from page 3, or downloaded in full colour from the RE Today website. A PowerPoint version of the 10 cards is also available for subscribers. Displaying each card on the whiteboard helps focus whole class feedback.

Time: Allow 15–20 minutes for whole class feedback.

(a) What, how and why do you celebrate?

- Place all the cards face up on the table.
- Ask children to take turns to tell their partner about something they 'celebrate' in their life or family. It might be a religious festival or a significant family event.
- Ask children to select cards from the pack that link to any of the things they do when they celebrate.
- Talk about: *What sorts of things in life are worth celebrating?* Ask children to record their ideas and have their reasons ready to share with the rest of the class.

(b) How and why do people celebrate religious festivals?

- Place the cards face down.
- Identify a religious festival the class is studying.
- Taking turns, each partner turns over a card and talks for 60 seconds about what they think that card has to do with how a particular religious festival is celebrated – for example how a Muslim family celebrates Eid; or a Christian family celebrates Easter or Christmas. Are there special foods, special ceremonies, for example, and if so what? (Adapt to suit the festival you are studying.) Use of a sand-timer or digital counter to mark out the 60 seconds helps children to focus.
- The listening partner decides if the topic has been well explained. If it has, the card is placed face down; if not the card remains face up. Pairs feed back their responses to the rest of the class.
- Gather information on the whiteboard under the following questions: What does the festival REMEMBER? What do people BELIEVE? How is the festival CELEBRATED today?
- As a class, identify together what is missing and what needs to be explored further. Agree how to do this.

RE Today weblink: www.retoday.org.uk

The cards on page 3 are available for download in full colour in the form of a PowerPoint presentation from the RE Today website for subscribers. (www.retoday.org.uk)

The password for access to the website can be found in each term's RE Today magazine.

For details of how to become a subscriber, see the RE Today website.

Using a song to engage children with a religious festival

For the teacher

The following activities use a song from one faith tradition as a stimulus for learning with 4–7 year olds. The focus here is on the Jewish festival of Succot, but the activities can be adapted to other religions.

Here we have used a song from religion, written for children. The language is accessible and the music engaging and enjoyable.

Religious music and songs as a resource in RE

- Songs from faith communities provide a real first hand resource. They can provide a 'window' into the religion.
- With a properly structured RE activity, children can enjoy, engage with and respond to the music and song and be stimulated into asking questions about religion.

Using songs from religions in RE and assembly

- Although there is often an overlap between Religious Education and Collective Worship in terms of some of the topics covered, they are two distinct areas of school planning and delivery. RE cannot be adequately delivered through Collective Worship. For example, a religious song in assembly may be used to encourage participation and give children a shared experience which supports their spiritual development. A song from religion used in Religious Education will need to be planned to provide a more rigorous learning experience to meet the requirements of the RE syllabus.

RE Today weblink:
www.retoday.org.uk

An MP3 file of the song. 'Lets build a Succah' by Stephen Melzack is available for download by subscribers from the RE Today website www.retoday.org.uk

I can ...

The following pupil-friendly criteria could be used to assess children's responses to the activities. Level 2 describes what most 7-year-olds should be able to do.

Level 1

- use **religious words to say** what a Succah is and how it is used today
- **talk about** who they would trust to lead them to safety when thinking about the Israelites following Moses through the desert.

Level 2

- be able to **retell** the story of Succot and say how Jews today celebrate Succot
- **express own ideas** about being brave and people to trust – linked to the story of the Israelites trusting God and following Moses

Links to Early Learning goals

Language for communication: listening with enjoyment and responding to stories, songs and other music.

Sense of community: understanding that people have different cultures and beliefs that need to be treated with respect.

For songs from other religions see for example:

Christianity

Come and Praise CDs from BBC (songs for collective worship drawn from the Christian tradition but with inclusive content).
The following CDs, made for worship, can be used with appropriate activities as resources in RE

- *Something Fischy* CD includes a track 'Whoa He's Alive' (Easter); Christian children's songs on http://fischy.com/shop/music-and-dvds/
- *Praise God with the Sticky Kids* on www.stickykids.net

Islam

- Song suitable for children about Eid: *Eid un Sa Eid un* by Zain Bhikhu; *Towards the Light* CD available from www.thenasheedshop.com
- *Expressions of Faith* CD of music and sounds from Islam for primary schools from Muslim Council of Britain:
www.mcb.org.uk/booksforschools.php

Exploring Succot through song activities

Information file

Succot is the festival which commemorates when the Jewish people wandered through the desert after the Exodus from Egypt and how God provided for them. They built temporary flimsy huts, Succahs, through which they could see the stars at night. The **Etrog** (Citron fruit) and the **Lulav** (three types of bound leaves – traditionally myrtle, willow and palm) are shaken together in all directions to symbolise sweetness and goodness.

Three activities using the song on page 7

Action song
- Provide children with tied bundles of leaves (to represent the Lulav) and large lemons (to represent the Citron fruit).
- Sing the song together.
- At appropriate points shake their Lulav or Citron fruit – up/down/left/right and in a circle).

Make and do

Build a Succah A Succah can be made by using a climbing frame and balancing branches over the top of the frame pre-strung with twine. Decorate with hanging fruit and vegetables. Role-play:
- the rabbi blessing the Succah – shaking the Lulav in all directions
- families eating and sleeping inside the Succah during the festival.

Jewish people often invite others to share a meal in their Succah. Ask the children to invite guests to their classroom Succah.

Make a 'shoebox' Succah: Children could create a mini Succah in a shoebox using Playmobil® people, leaves and cut-out fruits. They could use these to act out what a Jewish family might do at Succot.

Tell the story behind the festival

During the Jewish festival of Succot people remember the time the Jewish people travelled in the desert after escaping from slavery in Egypt, and how God looked after them. They had left all their possessions behind in Egypt. It was often hard and dangerous in the desert and they were often grumpy, but they trusted Moses their leader, and God to get them safely to a new land.

Tell children the story from the book of Exodus in the Bible using a child-friendly version. A good one is 'The Long Journey' by Bob Hartman in the *Lion Storyteller Bible*, ISBN 0 7459 3607 5.

Stop, think, question, share

In pairs, ask children to choose their favourite moment in the story. Gather suggestions and agree one moment to focus on.
Retell the story – **stop** at the key moment.

Think: Ask children to focus on Moses and think about the following four questions
- What is he doing?
- How is he feeling?
- What puzzles him? What question might he ask?
- If you could be there, what question would you ask?

Share: In turns each child shares their answers with a partner and then the group. Record responses on the whiteboard.

Personal reflection:
- What would you miss most if you had to leave your home quickly? What would you take?
- Who would you trust to lead you to safety?

Using song to engage children with a religious festival

Let's Build A Succah

Words and Music by Stephen Melzack
Arranged by Tim Smith

4-7

Let's build a suc-cah made of wood
Let's take the Lu-lav Et-rog too
Let's build a suc-cah All join in

Let's build a suc-cah Fill it up with fruit Has it got a roof? NO!
Hold them quite tight and This is what you do Shake them in the air YES!
Let's build a suc-cah Let the fun be-gin Hang-ing up the fruit YES!

We can see the sky Eat our meals and sleep in it
Shake them all a-round Suc-cot has ar-rived In the
Pic-tures on the wall Now the suc-cah's built Hap-py

Eve-ry sin-gle night Now the Suc-cah's built Hap-py Suc-cot one and all.
Suc-cah we'll be found
Suc-cot one and all

© Stephen Melzack, used with permission.

A song from *Two Candles Burn* by Stephen Melzack

This is one of the 10 songs exploring Jewish festivals on this CD. All 10 songs are carefully written to capture the essence of the festival and engage children in the 4–11 age group. The CD provides the words and backing track for use in the classroom. Available from the RE Today catalogue. (www.retoday.org.uk).

Using dance to engage children with a religious festival

For the teacher

The following activities use dance from one faith tradition as a stimulus for learning with 4–7 year olds. The focus here is on the Hindu festival of Navratri, but the activities can be adapted to other religions.

Religious music and dance as a resource in RE:

- Dance from faith communities provide a real first-hand resource. They can provide a 'window' into the religion.
- With a properly structured RE activity children can enjoy, engage with and respond to religion through the stimulus of music and dance.

Expectations and outcomes

The following pupil-friendly criteria could be used to assess children's responses to the activities. Level 2 describes what most 7-year-olds should be able to do.

Level 1

- name and use some religious words to talk about a festival that Hindus like to celebrate.
- *talk about how taking part in the stick dance made me feel and say why dancing is a good way to celebrate a religious festival.*
- *talk about ways of being kind and good and how it makes me feel when people are kind and caring to me.*

Level 2

- retell the story of Durga and talk about what some Hindus do to celebrate Navratri today.
- *create a dance which celebrates something happy and give my own thoughtful ideas about why dancing is a good thing to do at a religious festival.*
- *respond, with thoughts of my own, to ideas about good and bad in the Durga story and thoughtfully suggest some ways I can show kindness to others.*

Information file

Navratri

Navratri literally means 'nine nights'. It is followed by Dasshera-Dass (tenth night) which commemorates the night Rama killed the demon Ravana. Navratri is an important festival for Gujarati Hindus.

What is the story of Navratri?

- Navratri recalls the story of a time when the world was plagued with a great demon who was only conquered when all of the gods came together and contributed the best of their powers. Through this the goddess **Durga** was created, and she defeated the demon.
- The tenth night (Dasshera-Dass) commemorates the day Lord Rama returned from exile after having killed the demon Ravana.

Why is Navratri celebrated?

Both stories commemorate the triumph of good over evil. It is believed that the energy of the goddess can help people live in a pure and kind way.

How is Navratri commemorated?

Traditional folk dances of garba and dandya-raas commemorate Navratri. These dances are **puja** – an act of worship in praise of the goddess Durga.

- **Garba** is a circle and clapping dance around an image of the mother goddess.
- **Dandya-raas or stick dance** is performed using decorative sticks which are gently hit against each other following the rhythm of traditional songs.

Colourful costumes and vivid saris are part of the occasion, with everyone enjoying dressing up and coming together as a community.

Using dance to engage children with a religious festival

Navarati - introducing a Hindu festival through dance

5–7

For the teacher

Get dancing!

- Invite a Hindu visitor to come to school to teach pupils the Dandya Raas Dance, also known as the stick dance. Ideally this might be a parent or a member of the local community. Try contacting your local RE advisory service for information about contacts with the Hindu community.

- Alternatively, watch a video clip showing celebrations at Navratri and, in an open space, such as the school hall or outside, develop your own simplified version of the dance.

- This could begin with children moving in a circle and clapping steadily to a rhythm provided by a drummer keeping the beat of the music.

- Move on to 'dandia-raas', the stick dance. Start pupils off in small circles of 6–8, each holding a suitable stick. Ideally this would be a polished dandiya stick, but anything appropriate you have available can be used. Ask pupils to work out a simple dance, tapping their partners' sticks in time to the music as they move around in a circle. Once children have the idea make up two circles, one facing inwards, the other facing outwards. Make up a simple dance where the two circles move in opposite directions and children tap sticks with the person opposite, in time to the music.

Follow up activities

Use a picture

Show the children a picture of the Mother Goddess Durga. A bright colourful version, displayed on the whiteboard, is best. A search in the images section of your internet search engine should provide a selection. Durga is usually shown sitting on a tiger or a lion and holding many divine weapons to fight evil.

Tell the story

Tell the story of how Durga was created as the goddess of goodness to destroy evil, by bringing together all the powers of the other gods. A version of the story for teachers can be found on the Staffordshire Learning net storyboard site: http://www.sln.org.uk/storyboard/stories/h2.htm

Provide a multi-sensory focus for reflection

Display a picture of Durga, the mother goddess. Around it display a selection of typical gifts offered by worshippers at Navratri – for example coconuts, Indian sweets, flowers.
Explain to children that Hindus believe the goddess helps them to live in pure and kind ways.

Talk together about ways in which we can show kindness and care to others. Children record their suggestions on petal-shaped cut-outs. Link these together to make a garland of flowers. Add to display.

Dandiyas – short polished brightly painted sticks used in the stick dance

Using an artefact to explore a religious festival: Eid ul Fitr (Islam)

For the teacher

Artefacts are a useful way of providing opportunities for younger pupils to develop imagination, creativity and language skills.

Religious artefacts, used effectively, provide a great 'engaging device' or 'way in' to learning for children. Try hiding a religious symbol or object inside a feely bag and let children wonder, carefully touch, suggest good words to describe what they are feeling, ask questions and then have a guess at what's inside. They are soon eager to find out more, to notice the object in a picture or a story, and, most importantly, to begin to understand the deeper meaning of the object for a believer and the feeling of those who use it.

Artefacts feature strongly in most religious festivals. Here we suggest some activities using artefacts as a stimulus for learning about and from the Muslim festival of Eid ul Fitr. Similar approaches can be applied to festivals celebrated in other religions.

See also

Some useful additional resources include:

A Child's Eye View of Festivals 1: DVD for young children: Child's Eye Media (includes Eid ul Fitr), available from the RE Today publications catalogue (see www.retoday.org.uk/catalogue – online catalogue, Early Years section).

A Story for Eid: A Very Helpful Little Boy by Azra Butt, an online Big Book from the Lancashire Literacy site telling the story of Sultan, a Muslim boy, as he prepares for Eid. http://www.lancsngfl.ac.uk/curriculum/literacy/lit_site/html/fiction/bigbooks/helpfulboy/index.html.

Artefacts supplier: Articles of Faith is a leading supplier of religious artefacts and resources for education by mail order. www.articlesoffaith.co.uk.

Information file: Eid ul Fitr

- Eid ul Fitr is the festival which marks the breaking of the fast for Muslims at the end of Ramadan.
- It is a time for family and friends to get together and celebrate.
- The festival begins when the new moon is seen in the sky.
- During Eid, Muslims not only celebrate the end of fasting, but thank Allah for the help and strength that he gave them to keep the fast throughout the previous month.

Expectations and outcomes

Foundation Stage

These activities make a contribution to developing knowledge and understanding of the world through handling artefacts with curiosity and respect; and to creative development through using religious artefacts as a stimulus to thinking about and expressing meanings.

5–7 year olds

The following pupil-friendly criteria could be used to assess children's responses. Level 2 describes what most 7-year-olds should be able to do.

Level 1: I can...

- **use some religious words** to talk about why Muslims like to send Eid cards.
- **talk about** what I think it means to be 'blessed' and suggest some 'blessings' I enjoy.

Level 2: I can...

- **give some reasons** why Muslims celebrate Eid ul Fitr today
- **talk about** some ways in which hands are used to express feelings and beliefs in worship, and **thoughtfully suggest** some ways I can use my hands to show kindness to others.

More able children may be able to :

- **make a link** between a Muslim choosing to buy Eid cards that support good causes and the meaning of Eid. (Level 3).

Using an artefact to explore a religiuos festival: Eid ul Fitr

5-7

For the teacher

You will need enough Eid cards for each group of children to have a selection. These are available from suppliers of religious artefacts for schools or direct from the manufacturers. An internet search will reveal suppliers in the UK who may well provide you with some examples at discounted prices if you make a good case!

Activity

- Provide children with a variety of Eid cards. Talk together about when we send greeting cards and why.
- In pairs, ask children to explore the cards and talk together about the questions on Card 1. Share answers.
- Use Card 2 activities to help children think about what Eid means for Muslims, and to help them reflect on the 'blessings' in their own lives. For example, such blessings may include: being healthy; having someone who loves them; being able to come to school; having friends to play with; having food to eat.
- As with charity Christmas cards, Eid cards often help raise money for Muslim charities such as Islamic Relief. Activity 3 aims to help more able children make the link between celebrating festivals and doing good deeds.

Card 1
- What do you notice about these cards?
- Which one do you like the best? Why?
- What do you think these cards celebrate?
- What makes you think this?

Card 2

Eid Mubarak means 'blessed festival'.
- What do you think it means to be 'blessed'?
- What things make you feel blessed? How can we bless other people?
- On a blank card, draw a picture to show something lovely in your life and write some words about how this makes you feel.

Card 3
- Why do you think a Muslim might like to buy an Eid card which also helped people in need?
- What sort of 'blessings' might this bring to these people? Make a picture using words and pictures to show your answer.

Hands and worship

5-7

For the teacher

Hands are put together or held open or aloft in worship; extended as a sign of friendship; decorated, to express happiness, prosperity or beauty, in eastern weddings and festivals. These are just some of the many ways our hands act as symbols, conveying deeper meaning. The following activities focus on the theme of 'hands' as a starting point for learning about Eid and for reflection on how hands are often used to show others our feelings and beliefs.

Starter activity

Ask pupils to

- Talk about how we use our hands.
- Work in pairs and choose two ways we may use them to help and two ways we may use them to hurt.
- Illustrate different hand signals and ask pupils to guess what they are. How many different hand signals can they think of? What do they mean?
- Give pupils a copy of the Eid card illustration below. In pairs ask them to answer the following questions: What are the hands doing on this card? What do you think it means?
- Talk about how the hands show that the person is open to listening to God and to receiving his blessings at Eid.

Ask pupils to

- Talk about how hands can be used to worship. Why are our hands important in worship?
- How would we use our hands to praise someone? To thank someone?
- Why do you think some Muslims decorate their hands?

Celebrating Eid with mendhi patterns

- Display pictures of hands decorated with mendhi patterns.
- Explain how some Muslim women apply henna to their hands and feet to make traditional patterns to celebrate the festival of Eid. Talk about how decorated hands might help worshippers remember God during and after Eid.
- Children could decorate a hand outline with mendhi patterns.

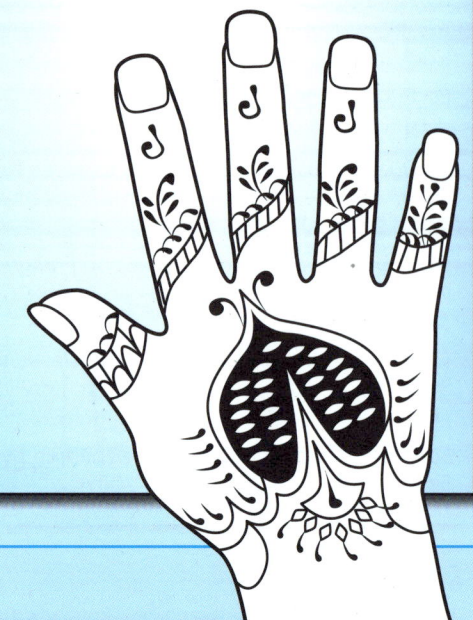

Using story and pictures to explore a religious festival (Easter: Christianity)

For the teacher

Faith stories are a key resource for Religious Education. The stimulus of a well-told, authentic faith story, linked to a properly structured task, will enable children to engage with, and respond to, some big ideas and questions at the heart of a religious festival.

The following activities use a story from one faith tradition as a stimulus for learning with 4–7 year olds.

The focus here is on the Christian festival of Easter, exploring the story behind the celebration of Good Friday and Easter Sunday. The approach can be adapted to suit other faith contexts. Teachers often express concern about tackling the story of the crucifixion and resurrection with young children. Here we share an effective strategy which has been shown to enable young children to

- engage with the story
- focus on the feelings of Jesus' friends
- use a structure for reflection to express their own times of sadness or happiness.

The activities make use of drama, pictures, story and music and link well with a range of cross-curricular strategies.

Resources

Lion Storyteller Bible by Bob Hartman, with illustrations by Susie Poole – excellent versions of Bible stories for telling aloud to younger children – Oxford: Lion Hudson 2001, ISBN 978-074593607-9.

Easter Journey, by Susie Poole, Pupfish ISBN 978-190463713-4.

RE Quest website: designed for use with and by children: www.request.org.uk/infants/festivals/easter/easter11.htm.

'How Do Christians Celebrate Good Friday?' 4-min video clip of a Good Friday service with a hymn and Bible reading: www.request.org.uk/infants/festivals/easter/easter01.htm. The story of Easter told interactively with pictures and spoken words for use by children.

Something Fischy' music CD for children by Stephen Fischbacher: http://fischy.com/2007/.

Expectations and outcomes

Foundation Stage

These activities make a contribution to developing personal, social and emotional development through exploring stories from religious traditions as a stimulus to reflect on their own feelings and experiences; and to communication, literacy and language development.

5–7 year olds

The following pupil-friendly criteria could be used to assess children's responses. Level 2 describes what most 7-year-olds should be able to do.

Level 1:
- **recall** the story of Mary on Easter Sunday
- **talk about** their own experiences and feelings of being sad and happy.

Level 2:
- **retell stories** connected with Easter and **say why** these are important to believers
- **ask questions and suggest answers** about stories to do with Easter
- **talk about** features in festival *stories that made people feel happy or sad and compare them with their own experiences.*

See also

BBC Watch series: Celebrations (5–7) available in E-book and Big Book versions. Christianity programme focuses on Easter. www.bbcactive.com/schoolshop/search.asp?

Classroom activities: Easter – a happy day

5-7

For the teacher

- **Getting started:** Seat pupils in a circle on the floor. Place lots of objects to do with Easter in the centre – e.g. Easter egg, loaf of bread, Easter card, Easter bunny, hot cross bun, palm cross, donkey, etc. Ask volunteers in turn to pick out one item and say what special time it is connected with.

- **Story:** Use the story and illustrations in 'A Happy Day' from *The Lion Storyteller Bible*, page 108, to retell the events of Easter Sunday.

- **Pictures:** Display the picture showing Mary and her friends at the start of the day. Talk about how Mary is feeling. Draw out responses from children which note how Mary Magdelene's sadness is illustrated by grey skies, holding on to others, tears. (A digital visualiser linked to your whiteboard is a great way of sharing pictures from books with the whole class.)

- Now show children the picture of Mary later in the day. Talk about how Mary is feeling now. Draw out responses from children which note how her happiness is shown by smiles, excitement, arms raised.

- **Drama:** In pairs children act out one such occasion – take it in turns to freeze-frame the action. Talk about how they feel and how their body language shows their feelings.

- Look at the pictures of Mary Magdelene again – how is she feeling? Why is she so happy? Use thought or speech bubbles alongside the pictures or a sentence starter beneath for pupils to complete.

- **Reflection:** Provide children with an opportunity to express their own thoughts and feelings by selecting a suitable structure to support this. The use of the cross in the activity on the next page reinforces children's learning about Easter at the same time as linking to their own experiences of sadness or happiness.

A sad day?

A happy day?

Illustrations © 2001 Susie Poole, taken from *The Lion Storyteller Bible* by Bob Hartman, published with the permission of Lion Hudson plc, 2001.

Using story and pictures

4–7

A structure for reflection: sad and happy crosses

- Talk about the feelings before and after Mary met Jesus.
- Link her feelings **before** to a time when children have felt sad. Identify the kind of things which make them sad and who or what helps them feel better.
- Link Mary's feelings **afterwards** with children's own ideas about celebrating good news, happy events. Identify together occasions when they have had good news and felt excited and happy.
- Have prepared some large plain cross shapes stuck on either bright (happy) or dark (sad) paper backgrounds. Invite children to choose either a sad cross or a happy cross and decorate the cross to show things which make them happy or sad, using words and pictures.

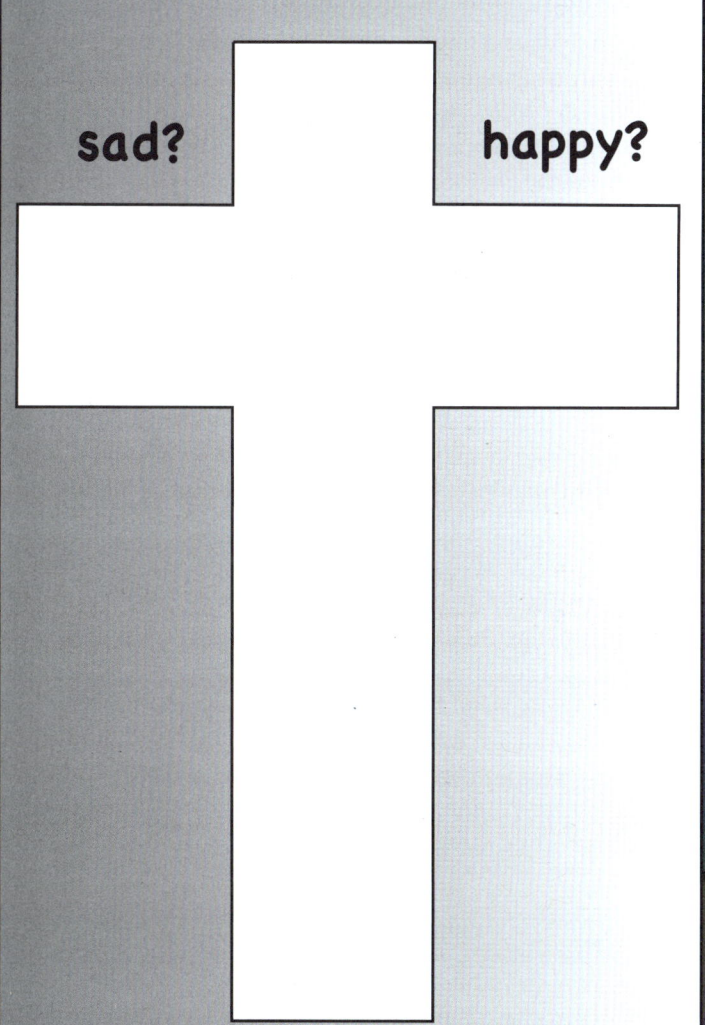

sad? happy?

An approach to the Easter story through music

Music is a great way of developing learning about religion and supporting children's own spiritual development.

The following music/video resources, designed for children, are a great way of 'getting inside' the meaning of Easter for Christians today.

Good Friday feelings

Show children the video clip 'How do Christians Celebrate Good Friday?' on the infant section of the RE Quest website (details on page 13).

Talk about:

- How are the people feeling?
- How do you know this? [Dark clothes; slow music; serious expressions]
- Who are they remembering?
- What special day do you think this is?

Easter Sunday feelings

On the screen show a large colour picture of Mary and her friends after seeing Jesus alive such as those shown here. Link these images to a Christian song for children such as: 'Whoa He's Alive' by Stephen Fischbacher, available on the CD *Something Fischy*. For details go to http://fischy.com/2007/.

Talk about:

Revisit the same questions as those above. Add the question:

- What had happened between Friday and Sunday to change their sadness into joy?

Bringing Easter alive: an Easter labyrinth

For the teacher

Easter in the RE curriculum

Across the primary school, a pupil is likely to encounter Easter as a key component of RE learning on many occasions. The Easter story is full of different angles and layers that allows it to stand up to this retelling; with careful planning it can grow up with the children who are hearing it.

Easter in the life of Christians

It is much harder to make it clear that this story plays a key role in the life of Christians and Churches. It is not celebrated widely in society as a whole, and with no fixed date in the calendar, it has fewer cultural associations that 'root' it into the understanding of pupils.

An approach for schools

- We called it a labyrinth: a kind of spiritual walk through the Easter events, with a focus on opportunities for spiritual development.
- At the heart of the approach is 'experience': the experience of meeting and hearing from Christians for whom Easter is important. This, linked with reflective learning experiences, enables pupils to go deeper into the Easter story, to learn from it and not just about it.

> In this section Pete Greaves, RE teacher and deputy head at Dovelands Primary School, a community school in Leicester, shares the approach he used to help children (and colleagues!) learn about and learn from Easter. Here he outlines his thinking behind the activities.

'The central aim was to secure understanding in the minds of pupils that Easter is a living festival in the lives of Christians and the local church. Meeting Christians, hearing them retell parts of the Easter story and taking part in reflective activities is at the heart of the approach.

'The local church was the venue, but if it hadn't been possible, the school hall would have worked. All 280 seven to eleven year olds took part over two mornings to accommodate them all. 'The physical act of the walk to church, followed by the atmosphere of the place of worship marked out the event as something special.

'As staff accompanied their classes, the labyrinth also provided a high level of INSET, enabling them to recognise the foundational nature of Easter within Christianity, as well as to experience some good learning activities to help pupils understand it.'

Pete Greaves

Expectations and outcomes

The following pupil-friendly criteria could be used to assess children's responses to the activities. Level 4 describes what most 11-year-olds should be able to do.

Level 3: I can...

- **express some understanding** of the different sections of the Easter story, **using appropriate vocabulary** such as 'betrayal, crucifixion, resurrection, etc.
- **show an understanding** of why the Easter story is important to Christians.

Level 4: I can...

- **offer some explanation** as to the motives and intentions of different characters in the Easter story
- **explain** the effect of a particular part of the Easter story on a believer's actions and share my own response to it.

Bringing Easter alive: an Easter labyrinth

Getting ready

7-11

The labyrinth

- A labyrinth in RE is a walk through time with experiences and responses linked to a theme. This one explored aspects of the Easter story – as presented by local Christian visitors and children's workers. It aimed to enable children to explore events in Holy Week in an interactive and stimulating way.
- Your labyrinth can have as many zones/phases stages as you like. It could have one for each 'stage of the cross', or you could pick out some significant parts of the story. For example:
  - Palm Sunday: Jesus arrives in Jerusalem
  - Jesus washes the disciples feet: perhaps exploring a theme of service/humility
  - The Last Supper: remembrance theme
  - Crucifixion: sacrifice theme
  - Empty tomb: resurrection theme.
- Time and resources will determine what you are able to do and quality will always have more impact than quantity.
- Once you have decided which parts you are going to focus on, carefully select an appropriate activity for pupils. Some could be 'experiential' activities based around art, video, photos, music or a mix of media. These would deepen pupils' experience of the event.
- The most significant experience, however, is meeting Christians who can share their faith and understanding.

Planning the event

- There are two keys to the success of the labyrinth – the setting and the guides.
  - **The setting:** Establish the setting for the labyrinth; consider how a particular environment will impact on the experience for pupils. If possible, go to the local church and make use of different spaces around the building.
  - **The guides:** Make contact with local Christians who can help. You may have contacts with the local church or with Christians who help out with assemblies. Seek out Christian families who will value the chance of sharing their lives with pupils.

Managing the event

- Get dates and timings in the school diary as soon as possible. No teachers like having things sprung on them, whatever the quality of the surprise.
- Mobilise support. Get a small working party together who can help you. Bring together enthusiastic staff members, governors and local faith community members, not forgetting to include support staff. A working lunch with food provided always gets volunteers!
- Plan out a 'timeline' that clearly sets out what arrangements need to be made between the planning stage and the final event. Don't forget to include things like letters to parents, set up times and a meeting with all those who are helping.

Getting the most out of the experience

Tips for teachers

- Think about how you are going to welcome groups to the beginning of the labyrinth. Have a clear start and end point, such as the lighting and extinguishing of a candle. Giving out a mini egg at the end does the trick too!
- Try to keep the labyrinth a kinaesthetic experience by not making any one activity too long. Fifteen minutes is probably the maximum time pupils can engage with a single part of the story if their attention is to be held.
- Build in time for moving around.
- Encourage session leaders to use the same structure as you would in a good quality lesson or assembly – with a beginning, middle and an end! Start by keying into pupils' current understanding; lead them through the story and then, finally, help them to reflect, perhaps by means of a question and a sharing of responses.
- Consider providing a 'memento' that pupils can take away with them for each part of the labyrinth. This will help them to remember the value of each section, rather than have it all end up as one big lump of memory mush at the end!

Back in the classroom

- Encourage staff to set aside plenty of time afterwards to enable pupils to express their responses.
- Give examples of engaging, expressive and reflective follow-up activities that will enable pupils to play to their strengths. A class set of recounts will rob the experience of much of its value!
- Secure a prominent display board so that pupil responses can be shared with the whole school community alongside as many photos as possible.

Most importantly of all, make sure you have bought yourself a huge Easter Egg so you can tuck into it when it's all over!

'Pupil reaction was overwhelmingly positive. There was a clear depth to the understanding of Easter and its importance for believers which I think was a key difference. Some responses were clearly focused on what Easter means to Christians, not just re-telling of the Easter story.'

Teacher

'We learnt about fears in the story of Easter, and our own fears. All in all we had a superb time and learnt about Easter in an action packed, exciting morning. We were sorry to return to school – but we needed our lunch!'

Year Six pupil

Dovelands pupils explore the meaning of 20 different crosses

Bringing Easter alive: an Easter labyrinth

Four example activities that have worked successfully as part of Easter labyrinth for 7-11 year olds:

Palm Sunday – Who is this man?

- **Getting started**: Talk about greetings around the world in different cultures. Explore how the way you greet someone tells of how you feel about them.
- **The story:** Share how Jesus was greeted as a king by those shouting praise and waving palm leaves. Also there were Pharisees who decided that they wanted to kill Jesus.
- **Something to think about:** How can you make decisions about whether someone is a good person or not? What question would you have asked Jesus to help you decide?
- **A memento:** Palm crosses that call to mind both the praise and the Pharisees.
- **Follow up focus:** Welcome for the King: The crowd welcomed Jesus as the Messiah who would change their lives and the world they lived in. What hopes and dreams did they have? What hopes and dreams do you have?

Personal responses from Doveland's pupils

Don't Forget...

The Last Supper – Will you follow?

- **Getting started**: Talk about jobs you hate doing and how good it would be if you could have a servant do all the nasty jobs.
- **The story:** Share how Jesus washed the disciples' feet and then shared the Last Supper. Talk about the themes of servant-hood and remembrance.
- **Something to think about:** Can pupils think of how these events would help Christians to remember Jesus and what he wanted them to do?
- **A memento:** A foot-shaped 'Post-it'® note with 'don't forget' written on it.
- **Follow-up focus:** Write a logo on the foot-shaped Post-it® note to sum up the message Jesus was demonstrating when he washed the disciples' feet. With a partner write down 10 acts of kindness they could do for others (service).

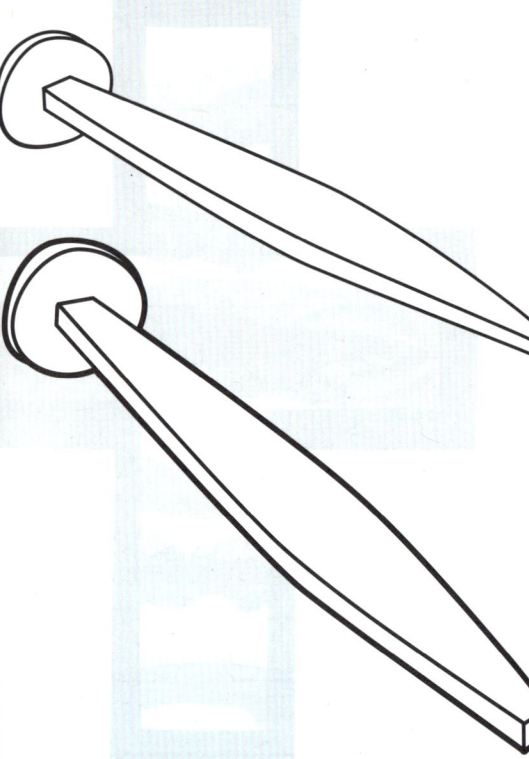

The crucifixion – What shall we do with him?

• **Getting started:** Ask pupils to think about a good day, a bad day and a really bad day they may have had. What makes a bad day into a really bad day?

• **The story:** Share the story of Good Friday from Peter's point of view with betrayal, Pilate's sentence and the crucifixion in age-appropriate detail.

• **Something to think about:** Remind them of Pilate's question, 'What shall we do with him?' What do Christians do with this story? Have they any clues as to why this might be called, 'Good Friday'?

• **A memento:** A nail – taking into account appropriate safety considerations.

• **Follow-up focus:** 'Good' Friday: Look at some 'Friday crosses' – which show the crucifixion and some 'Easter crosses' which are empty to show the resurrection. Consider why Christians find Easter hopeful, and their own ideas about hope.

The resurrection – Where is he?

• **Getting started:** Ask pupils to think about the week the disciples had experienced. What would have been their high point so far? What about their low point?

• **The story:** Share the story of the resurrection.

• **Something to think about:** Show some different types of crosses some with Jesus on the cross and others without. Talk about the differences between the 'Good Friday' crosses and the 'Easter Sunday' crosses. Why might both be important for Christians? Can they think why Christians think the resurrection of Jesus is good news for them today?

• **A memento:** A sunflower seed to be planted.

• **Follow-up focus:** Design and make a 'resurrection' sculpture, window or painting showing their learning about Christian understandings of new beginnings and hope for the future.

See also.....

If you would like to try an approach like this but would like more detailed guidance look at:

Experience Easter with Children, produced by Shahne Vickery, Catherine Coster, Janet Lunt and Carolyn Wright. This pack provides guidance to help children experience the Easter story through six easy to assemble, interactive stations set up in different parts of the church. It includes detailed instructions to church members to enable them to create the stations, and instructions to help school group leaders introduce and reflect on each part of the story. Published by Jumping Fish, price £12.00, available from Diocese of Gloucester Resource Centre, 9 College Green, Gloucester GL1 2LX.
Tel 01452 835559 Email: jumpingfish@glosdioc.org.uk.

Celebrating Divali: Hindu and Sikh perspectives

For the teacher

The lesson ideas in the following pages focus on the festival of Divali and what it means to Hindus and Sikhs. Although some of the festival activities are shared, the festival stories are different, as is the meaning and impact on individuals. The two resources provided on pages 22 and 24 are first person recounts from a Hindu and a Sikh about how they celebrate Divali and what it means to them. These provide authentic insights into the festival, and support pupils in understanding the significance of the festivals for individuals, as well as encouraging them to reflect on their own times of celebration, and some fundamental and shared values e.g. freedom.

Curriculum links

The Year 4 non-fiction Unit 1 of the Literacy Framework in England can be purposely linked to other areas of the curriculum. These resources provide an excellent RE stimulus for such literacy work; they also support the QCA's RE unit of work: 'How and why do people celebrate religious festivals?'

Expectations and outcomes

The following pupil-friendly criteria could be used to assess children's responses to the activities. Level 4 describes what most 11-year-olds should be able to do.

Level 3: I can....
- **recognise** the similarities and differences between the Hindu and Sikh festivals of Divali
- **make links** between the Divali festival stories and experiences of my own.

Level 4: I can.....
- **describe** some similarities and differences between the Hindu and Sikh festivals of Divali
- **ask and answer questions** about the Divali festival stories, referring to the beliefs of the religion.

See also

There is a wealth of material on Divali – the resources mentioned here represent some of the best:

1. *Celebrations and Special Times* (BBC 2007): an excellent whiteboard active resource pack (CD-ROM), containing video clips, classroom activities and teacher's book. Hindu Divali only. www.whiteboardactive.com.
2. *The Divali Story (Hindu): Special Times*, ed Joyce Mackley, RE Today 2004, ISBN 978-1-904024-52-1, www.retoday.org.uk
3. *Divali in Leicester* (Hinduism) video: www.bbc.co.uk/leicester/videonation/archive/a_f/dipak_joshi_my_diwali.shtml.
4. **Five Days of Divali** – Five video clips: www.bbc.co.uk/asiannetwork/features/diwali.shtml.
5. **The Divali Story (Sikh):** www.allaboutsikhs.com/Main/Bandi-Chhor-Divas.html
6. **Divali for Hindus, Sikhs and Jains:** www.bbc.co.uk/birmingham/faith/2003/10/diwali_festival_of_light.shtml.
7. **QCA unit of work for Year 4** 'How and why do people celebrate religious festivals?': www.qca.org.uk/qca_12164.aspx

My Hindu Divali

Hello! My name is Bharti and I am a Hindu. Divali is a special time of year for me. Let me tell you about it.

Preparations for my Divali celebrations begin in earnest after Vijaya Dasmi, when I start cooking the traditional food, cleaning the house, planning the rangoli patterns, buying the decorations and searching out the divas.

I clean the house from top to bottom in readiness for goddess Lakshmi and for all the guests who will visit. A week before, I put up decorations, and every evening from four days before, I carefully place lighted divas at every door in the house, as well as outside the front door. Rangoli patterns are also made and placed at the door.

Two days before Divali is known as Than Teras. On this day Lakshmi Puja is done and, following tradition, I wash coins in a ritualistic way, say prayers and hope that goddess Lakshmi will bless me with enough wealth to meet all my needs in the coming year.

On Divali day I say prayers at the home shrine in the morning and at dusk, and then have a party in the evening. Each person is greeted at the door and offered a dish of sweets and spices. We go outside and light the fireworks and then come in and share a hot vegetarian meal. We party until midnight and then greet each other with "Happy New Year" before departing.

On New Year's Day I try and go to the Temple to take part in the Annakut Mahotsav, but the Temple is 22 miles away so I cannot always go. I visit the homes of friends and family, exchanging New Year greetings and eating all the special dishes cooked for Divali!

Bharti Tailor

Bharti Tailor

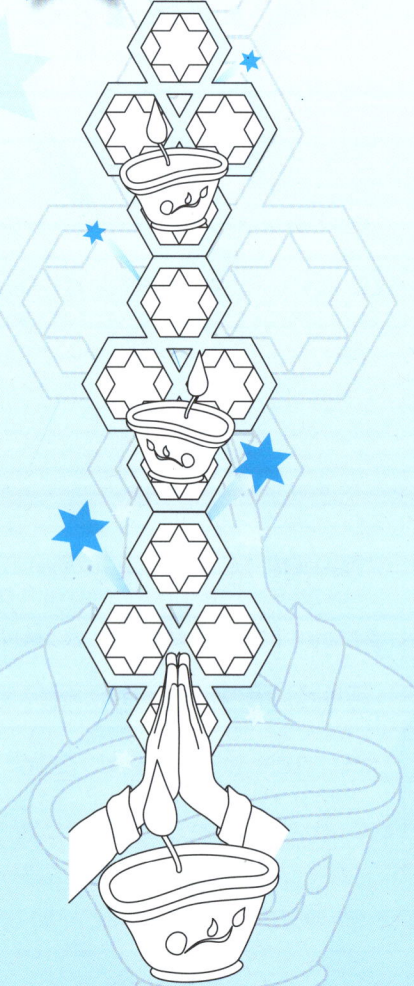

© 2008 RE Today Services
Permission is granted to photocopy this page for use in classroom activities in schools that have purchased this publication.

Celebrating Divali: Hindu

7–11

1. Why is Divali so important to Bharti?

This activity is designed to get pupils to answer the question: Why does Bharti spend so much time and effort getting ready for Divali? You will need to provide a set of the six cards below for each pair/group of pupils. Ask pupils to:

- **read carefully** Bharti's personal recount of Divali
- **sort** the six statements about Divali (see below) into an order of priority – with the one Bharti might think is most important at the top
- **prepare** an oral report to answer the question: Why does Bharti spend so much time and effort getting ready for Divali? They should use key terms e.g. diva, Lakshmi, puja, rangoli.
- **present** their report to the class. If time and resources are available this could be recorded as a sound file or podcast, and published on the school network.

2. How are Hindu and Sikh Divali celebrations similar ... and different?

If you are covering more than one festival then this activity provides an opportunity for pupils to compare different festivals, their meanings and the religions from which they come; it is also a powerful way of reinforcing and extending learning. Ask pupils to:

- **complete the writing frame** on page 26. The names of two festivals are already filled in – pupils should write in the name of the third, e.g. a festival they celebrate themselves, or one they have studied in RE.
- **identify** what the three festivals share, what is shared by two of the three festivals, and what is unique to each. They record their answers on the writing frame.
- **feedback** to the class, and add any new ideas gained to their record.

Divali is a time for family and friends to get together and enjoy themselves.	Hindus all over the world – Sikhs and Jains too – celebrate Divali at the same time, which is a wonderful feeling.	Divali marks the start of a new year, and is a time for making new resolutions to please God.
Divali is a time to pray to God, to ask God to provide all you need to live and be happy in the new year.	Divali is a time to tell the festival story, to be reminded of its meaning for people today.	Most Hindus think they should celebrate Divali even if they are not too sure of the religious stories behind it.

© 2008 RE Today Services
Permission is granted to photocopy this page for use in classroom activities in schools that have purchased this publication.

My Sikh Divali

Hello! My name is Butta and I am a Sikh. Sikhs do not celebrate Divali, but the Sikh celebration of **Bandi Chor Divas** takes place at the same time so there are many similarities between the two festivals. Let me tell you about it.

As a Sikh I celebrate Divali because it was on that day in 1619 that Guru Hargobind Sahib arrived at Amritsar after he and 52 princes had been released from Gwalior prison. On that day, the Golden Temple was lit up with many lights to welcome him home and to celebrate his release. Ever since then Sikhs have continued this annual celebration by lighting lamps outside Gurdwaras and giving out sweets to everyone. Sikhs call this special day of remembrance **Bandi Chor Divas**. The word 'Bandi' means 'imprisoned', 'Chor' means 'release' and 'Divas' means 'day', and together 'Bandi Chor Divas' means **Prisoners' Release Day**.

We get ready for Bandi Chor Divas at home and at the Gurdwara.

At home:

- Candles are lit to highlight that good will always overcome evil
- Fireworks are lit in celebration
- Prayers are read in remembrance of this time in Sikh history
- Prayer is said to God to help us in our everyday struggle with evil.

At the Gurdwara:

- Candles and fireworks are lit in celebration
- Prashad is distributed, welcoming everybody and anybody into the Gurdwara
- Indian sweets which have been offered to the Guru are shared with everyone
- Langar (free food which is vegetarian) is served to make us understand that we are all are equal
- Prayers are said with everyone to God to help us not make mistakes.

Butta Singh

Butta Singh

Celebrating Divali: Sikh

Classroom activities: my Sikh Divali

7–11

1. Why does Butta celebrate Divali?

Give pupils a copy of the account 'My Sikh Divali' on page 24. Ask them to work in pairs to:

- **highlight** any words or phrases that show why Butta celebrates Divali
- **agree a sentence** to answer the question: 'Why do Sikhs celebrate Divali?'

2. Exploring Divali as a celebration of freedom

Explain that the name 'Divali' comes from the ancient Sanskrit word 'Deepavali' meaning 'row of lights'. Ask pupils to:

- **suggest** why a 'festival of lights' is a good way of celebrating a festival of freedom
- **complete** a spider diagram around the word 'Freedom' to show what freedom means and why it is something to celebrate.

3. An organisation that works for freedom

Sit pupils in a circle, and soften any lighting. Ask them to relax and sit very still. A stilling exercise is useful here.

- **Read** the story behind the festival of Bandi Chor Divas (see below) and ask pupils to suggest what the story says about 'freedom' and 'justice'.
- **Show** pupils a candle inside a coil of barbed wire. Light the candle, and ask children to say the thoughts and questions that come to their mind. **Explain** that it is the symbol of Amnesty International, an organisation that exists today to help people whose freedom has been taken away for unfair reasons
- **Ask pupils to draw** an outline of the candle surrounded by wire, and to **record** key words and ideas about freedom and justice around it.
- **Ask pupils to decide** – Would Butta support Amnesty International? Why or why not?

The story behind Sikh Divali – Bandi Chor Divas

In the time of the sixth Guru, Guru Hargobind, the Emperor became very ill. He was told that he would only recover if a holy man prayed for his good health. The Emperor asked Guru Hargobind to stay in the fort at Gwalior to pray for his recovery.

This fort was also a prison, and whilst Hargobind was treated well, he was angered by how badly the prisoners were treated. Fifty-two Hindu princes had been unfairly imprisoned there. They were not given enough to eat and wore only rags. Hargobind did all he could to help them, but it was when the Emperor recovered and ordered his release that he saw his opportunity.

Guru Hargobind told the Emperor that he would not leave without the other prisoners. The Emperor could not understand the Guru and did not want to free the prisoners – but told him he could take as many prisoners as could hold on to his coat as he left.

The Emperor thought this would be only three or four at the most. Imagine his surprise when the Guru left with all 52 prisoners! The Guru, determined to help all of them, had made himself a very long cloak with 52 tassels. Each prisoner held onto a tassel and walked to freedom behind the Guru.

Guru Hargobind leads the 52 princes to freedom

Two different Divali celebrations – exploring similarities and differences

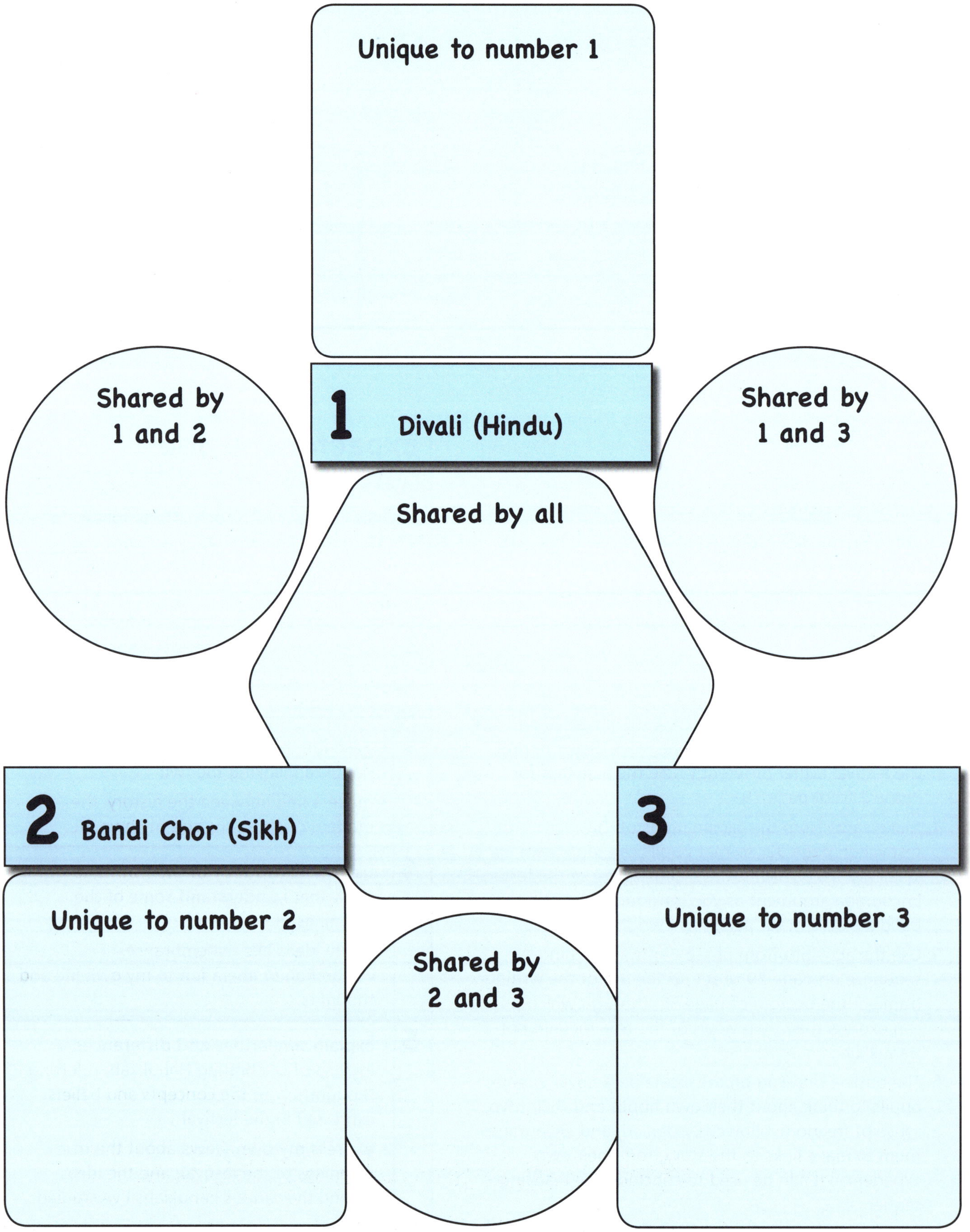

Unique to number 1

1 Divali (Hindu)

Shared by 1 and 2

Shared by 1 and 3

Shared by all

2 Bandi Chor (Sikh)

3

Unique to number 2

Unique to number 3

Shared by 2 and 3

26 © 2008 RE Today Services
Permission is granted to photocopy this page for use in classroom activities in schools that have purchased this publication.

Hanukkah: what's the real meaning of this Jewish festival?

9–11

For the teacher

Hanukkah is commonly taught in RE for pupils aged 7 to 10. The following activities enable pupils to learn from Judaism as well as learning about the festival of Hanukkah, whilst integrating persuasive writing aspects of literacy.

The suggestions seek to

- integrate the learning sequence of the renewed literacy strategy into the RE work
- enable teachers to use RE guided writing work to assess achievement in both RE and literacy.

For teachers using the renewed literacy framework in England, it fits well into Year 5: other teachers may use it more flexibly.

Teaching sequence and learning activities

1. Tell the Hanukkah story to the class. Get them to study the text of Thaddeus's story (page 28).
2. Use activities selected from Phase one on page 29 to fix the story, and open it up for exploration by the pupils.
3. Show the pupils the four different hanukiahs (pages 30-31) and discuss the ways they symbolise the meanings of the festival. Ask them who would like each one and why. Consider the ways they interpret the festival rather differently. Use the activities for Phase 2 from page 29.
4. Make cards from the explanations of the festival on page 32, so that pupils can rank them in small groups: Which is the real meaning of the festival? Encourage argument as you introduce this task, to build a platform for persuasive writing later on.
5. Use the activities from phase 3 of the teaching sequence on page 29 to set up the use of the writing frame at the bottom of page 32, through which pupils can express their own views of the true meaning of Hanukkah.
6. The outline drawing on the inside back cover enables pupils to think about their own hopes and their own sense of freedom, allowed or denied, and encourages them to make links to the story from their own experience. It can be used to conclude the teaching sequence.

Expectations and outcomes

If pupils can say yes to some of the following 'I can...' statements then they are showing evidence of achievement at the levels indicated.

I can...	
2	• **identify** some features of celebration • **respond sensitively** to the emotions of the Hanukkah story.
3	• **describe** the story and celebrations of Hanukkah, linking the two • **make a link** between the history, the modern celebrations and my own life.
4	• **use the vocabulary** of the festival to show that I **understand** some of the meanings of Hanukkah • **apply ideas** like remembrance, celebration or liberation to my own life and thoughts.
5	• **explain similarities and differences** in ways of celebrating Hanukkah, referring thoughtfully to the concepts and beliefs expressed in the festival • **express my own views** about the true meanings of the festival, and the ideas behind the various hanukiahs I've studied.

Thaddeus' story of Hanukkah

This narrative from 164 BCE is told from the viewpoint of a child.

People are going to be celebrating this week for centuries to come. I'm Thaddeus, I'm 11, and I want to tell you about what happened in the Temple this autumn. We have been stamped on for so long by the Greeks that I can't believe what has happened. After all these years when they turned our wonderful Temple into a pigsty, we've got it back!

Antiochus is the evil Greek ruler over our land. He has been trying to stamp out Jewish faith for years. We have been forbidden to practice our religion by laws and terrorised by his soldiers, but you can only keep people down for so long – the urge to be free is strong. Three years ago, he took over our temple, and turned it into a place of worship to himself! He is so proud – he even calls himself 'Obviously god'! But Judah Maccabee, our leader, has given him a hammering now, and we have won our temple back. No one really thought our fighters could beat the armies of Antiochus, but they fought like men inspired. My dad is one of the fighters with Judah Maccabee, and he says Judah is the cleverest, bravest and most dedicated leader since King David himself.

Our fighters have taken back the Temple, and the city of Jerusalem. Jewish people can be proud of their faith once again! When we threw out all the foul and filthy stuff and cleaned it all up, the Almighty blessed us with a miracle. It's amazing! We wanted to light the menorah, the huge candle lamp stand, but there was only a tiny bit of clean oil to burn in it. Well, Judah had it lit up anyway. It might have been enough oil for one night, but it burned, and burned for eight whole nights. It's a kind of sign that the Eternal is with us. Everybody has been going to the Temple, not just to celebrate the victory or to praise the Holy One, but also to stare at the lamp that keeps burning by a miracle! I went to the Temple myself. The last time I had been there was when I was eight, and it was dreadful, because the Greek soldiers were all defiling it and spoiling everything. Last week, Dad took me up the Temple Mount, and we walked in through the courtyards. There were Jewish people everywhere, singing the old songs, cheering for Judah and the fighters, and sweeping, cleaning, washing and making the place beautiful for worship again. I joined in. I loved it. We didn't go home till really late.

As I said at the beginning, people will never forget this. I wonder what they will most remember? Perhaps it will be the fighting, or maybe the wonderful work of God. Possibly it will be the freedom we feel today. Maybe they will just sit at home in families and tell the whole story, again and again, into history? Whatever happens, Jews will always remember this, I'm quite sure...

Hannukah: the meaning of the Jewish festival

Classroom activities: a teaching sequence about Hanukkah based on the literacy framework

7–11

Phase one
Familiarisation with the text

Prior learning: Pupils may already know something about Judaism, and about festivals more generally.

Begin by telling the story of Hanukkah to the class. To build on this, set tasks for pupils to explore and understand the narrative. In groups pupils could tackle some of the following:

- Fill in a 'senses grid': What did Thaddeus see, hear, smell, touch, feel in the story?
- Create sound effects to accompany five or six key moments in the story.
- Choose and list ten 'props' they would use to dramatise the story.
- Cast a movie: If this story was to be filmed, which actors would you have in each role, and why? Who would make a good Antiochus, Judah, Thaddeus?
- Make an emotional graph of Thaddeus' feelings through the story.

RE Today weblink:
www.retoday.org.uk
The RE Today subscribers' website has a free download, a PowerPoint presentation in which some of these activities are introduced to pupils. if you're a subscriber, check *REtoday* for your password and help yourself to this.

Phase two
Capturing ideas

Exploring the true meaning of Hanukkah.

Pupils model and share their responses, with a view to beginning to write an argument or persuasive piece. A teacher's involvement will vary in different groups around the class.

Ask pupils to:

- talk about the four examples of hanukiahs, answering 'who, what, where, when, why' about them, in groups and then for the whole class.
- in pairs give four different ideas (single words or phrases) about each of the hanukiahs: what do they mean?
- put images of the four hanukiahs on the wall or whiteboard. Ask pupils to defend their viewpoint about which hanukiah expresses the meaning of the festival best.
- consider the different possible alternative 'real meanings' of the festival with care and clarity.

Phase three
Guided writing for assessment in RE and literacy

This task aims to enable pupils to write a persuasive piece, for a website, defending their view of 'The real meaning of Hanukkah.'

- Begin with some modelling: show pupils the accounts on page 32 and ask them to think about how they are the same and how they differ.
- Which of the four families would you choose to visit at Hanukkah? How would Hanukkah be different in each? Discuss and rank your answers.
- Pupils might consider Thaddeus' story. Is it well written? Does it persuade people to his point of view? How could it be better?
- Use the writing prompt sheet (page 32) to develop, draft and redraft a piece of persuasive writing that is about 150–200 words long. The subject of the work is: 'What is the true meaning of Hanukkah?'
- Pupils may find that using the outline on the inside back cover helps them to clarify their own thoughts about hope and freedom.

Four Hanukkah lamps

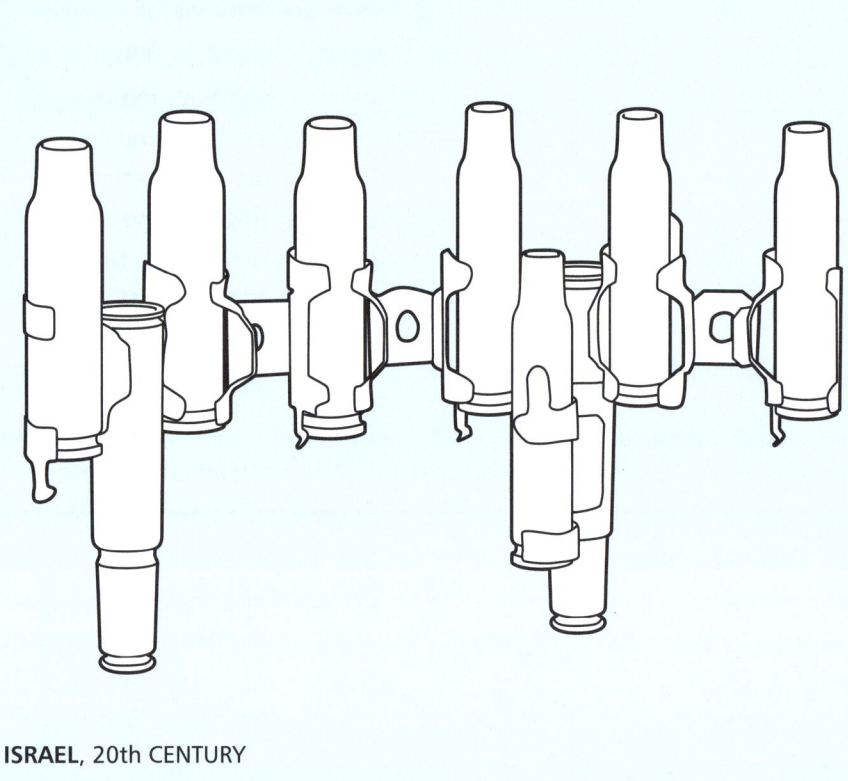

ISRAEL, 20th CENTURY

This hanukiah is made from bullet cases from the 1967 Yom Kippur War.

For some Jews, Hanukkah is a festival of freedom won by fighting for their faith. This links the ancient story of the Judah Maccabee with modern Israel. The modern country has been at war with some of its neighbours.

- Is the meaning of Hanukkah different for different people?
- Does the meaning of the festival change from age to age?
- Is it a festival of war, or of peace?

This hanukiah is nearly 200 years old.

The crown at the top is a symbol of the power of the Almighty, and the pillars and doors are reminders of the temple and the Torah scrolls. It is made of silver. There is a tiny jug to fill the oil lamps and a candlesnuffer for when the lights are put out.

- Who would like this hanukiah best?
- Is the festival mostly about the traditions and the history of Jewish life?

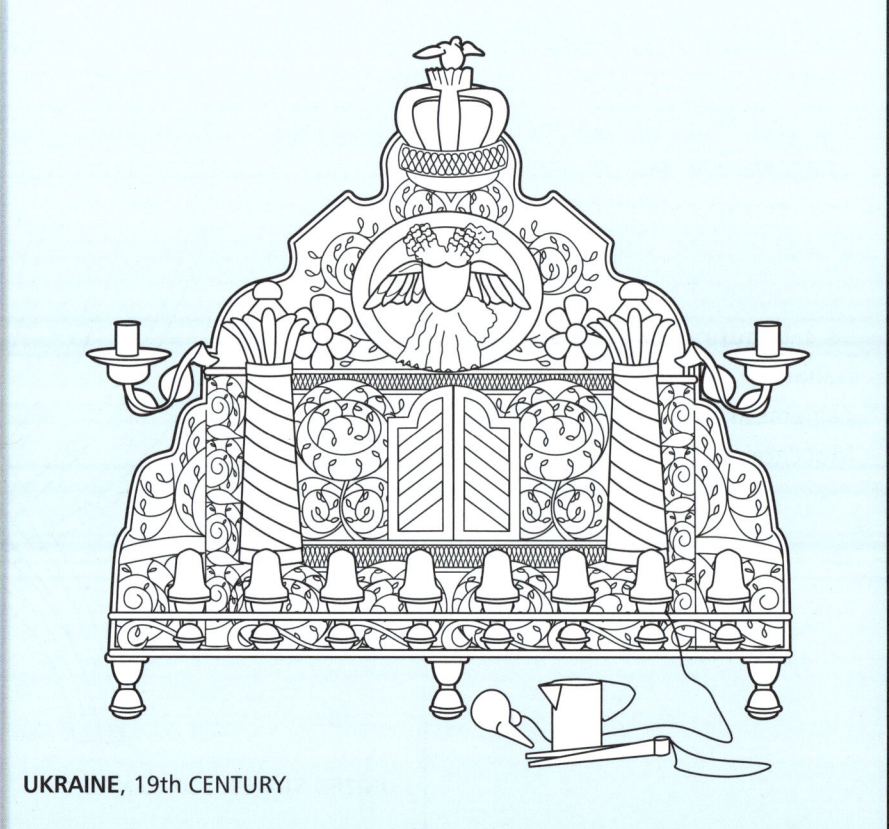

UKRAINE, 19th CENTURY

Hannukah: the meaning of the Jewish festival

7-11

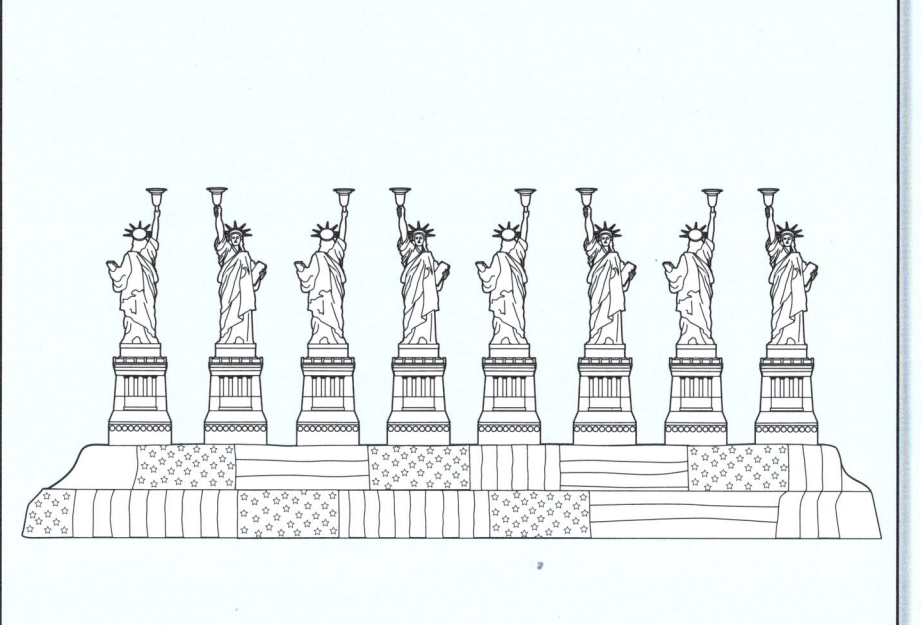

UNITED STATES, 1974

There are millions of Jewish people who live in America. This hanukiah was made by May Shafter Rockland in 1974. It uses eight small plastic replicas of the statue of Liberty, America's famous symbol of freedom, as the candleholders for Hanukkah.

- Who would like this hanukiah best?
- Is the festival about the same kind of freedom as the statue of liberty?
- Do you think American Jews might feel differently about the festival from Jewish people who live in Britain or in Israel?

This modern silver style of candleholder was made by the artist Ludwig Wolpert. It shows one way of linking the ancient celebrations of Jewish people with modern approaches to art and craft.

Is a beautiful and artistic hanukiah the best way to remember the story of Judah Maccabee?

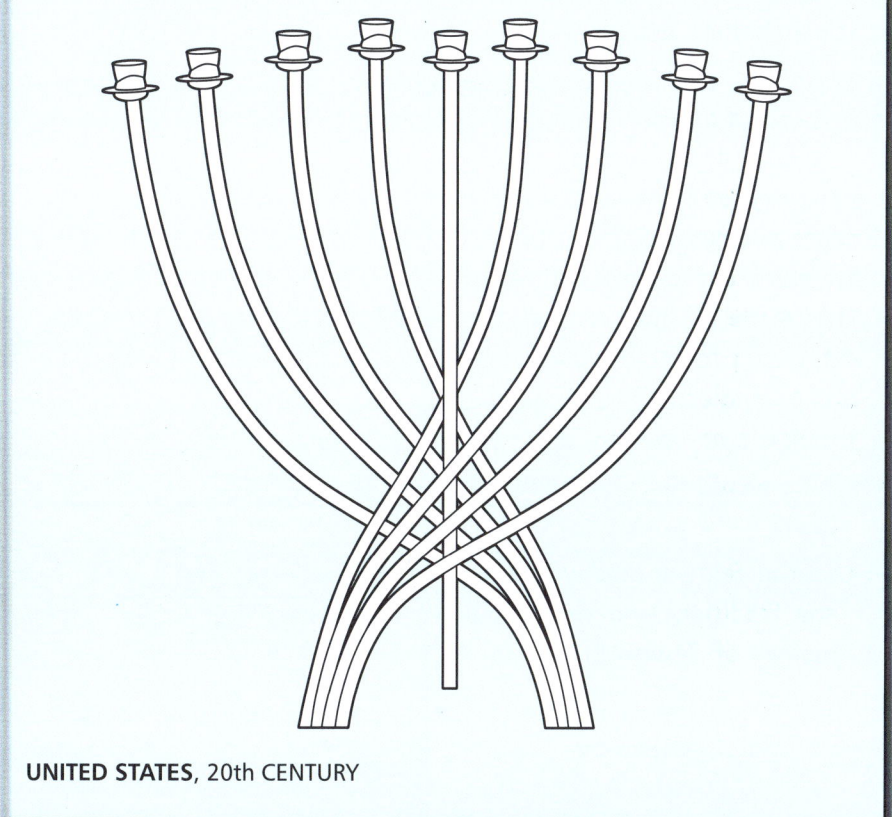

UNITED STATES, 20th CENTURY

© 2008 RE Today Services
Permission is granted to photocopy this page for use in classroom activities in schools that have purchased this publication.

What does Hanukkah mean?

Different people see different meanings in the festival. Here are four Jewish explanations of the festival.

Quote A: 'In our family, when it's Hanukkah, we remember the bravery of Judah Maccabee and we sing songs that remind everyone in the story. You have to light one candle each night, so that by the end of the festival, all eight will be burning together. For us, it's a family festival: everyone tries to be home for Hanukkah. Just as Judah dedicated the temple afresh to God, so we dedicate ourselves to be faithful observers of all the Law. I'd say it's a festival of dedication.'	**Quote B:** 'Our Hanukiah is very special because it belonged to our grandfather. He fled from the Nazis in Germany, and he brought it with him in the 1930s when he first came to England. Judah Maccabee had to struggle to survive and be free 2100 years ago. Our grandfather had to struggle free too. We remember him when we light his candlestick. It makes us talk about him, and swap old stories. For us, Hanukkah is a festival of freedom.'
Quote C: 'What we like most about Hanukkah is lighting the lights. It happens in our town about the same time as Hindu Divali, and Christian Christmas. They are festivals of light as well, so we are happy to have a Jewish celebration to enjoy. The miracle of the lamps in the cleaned out temple is a great story. A festival of lights is a time to think of the power and love of the Almighty. He lights up our lives all year long.'	**Quote D** 'In 1967, there was a war in which the Jewish people of Israel had to fight for their survival. My uncle was in the Israeli army then, and was wounded. We always remember this at Hanukkah, and we try to make sure that we honour those who may be fighting for their faith today. Hanukkah is a festival of liberation. People who want to be free in their own land still have to fight for it.'

Writing about the real meaning of Hanukkah

You are going to contribute to a website for people who are learning about the Jewish religion. Your piece of writing must argue the case for what you think is the real meaning of Hanukkah. Here are some prompts to help you write persuasively about the real meaning of the festival.

Describing: • At Hanukkah, Jewish people remember … • The festival started when … • These days, the celebrations include … • The most important thing about the festival is …	**Explaining:** • The meaning of the Hanukiah lamps is … • There are different ideas about the meaning of the festival such as … • The festival has lasted for over 2000 years. Maybe this is because …
Persuading: • I think the main meaning of the festival is … • Some people say… but I disagree because … • The reason for my opinion is …	**Convincing** • My view of the meaning is right because … • I'm sure that what matters most is … • The main emphasis of the festival has to be …

WORD BANK

Words that describe the story: freedom / fight / miracle / family / temple / dedication / liberating

Words that might describe the festival today: celebrate / festival / remembrance / pride / tradition / energy / family occasion / community

Words that you might use to persuade people about your view of the festival: disagree / significant / important / emphasis / argument / experience

32 © 2008 RE Today Services
Permission is granted to photocopy this page for use in classroom activities in schools that have purchased this publication.